THINGS MEDICAL ASSISTANTS Really WANT TO Say But Can't

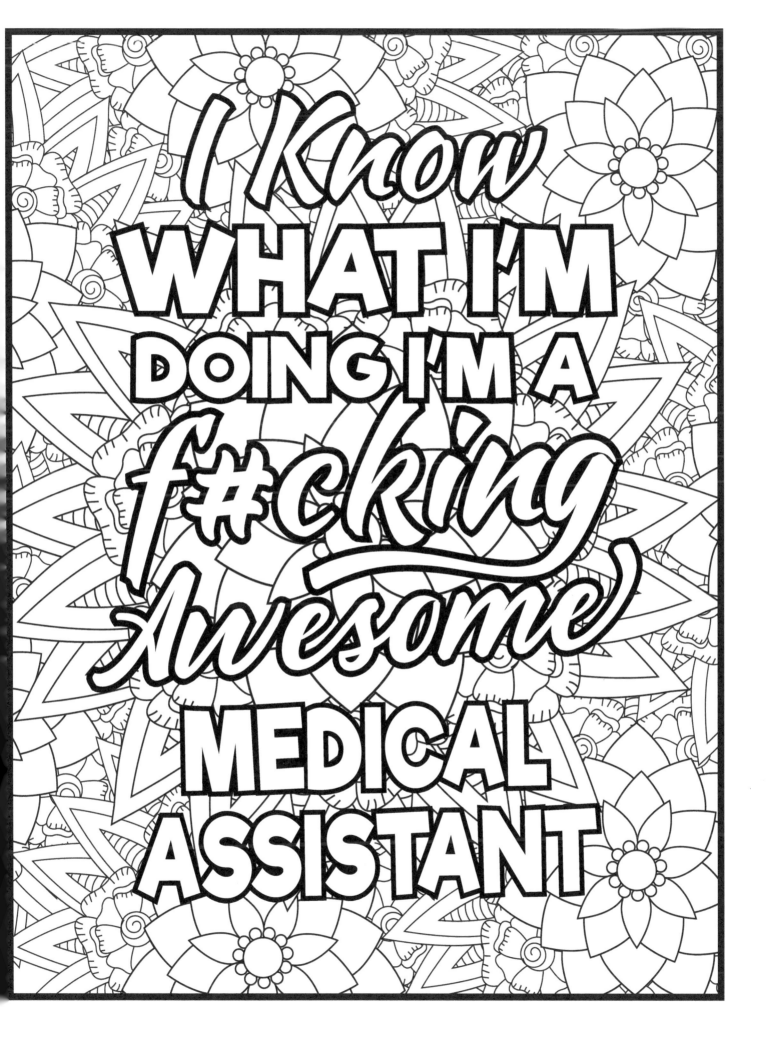

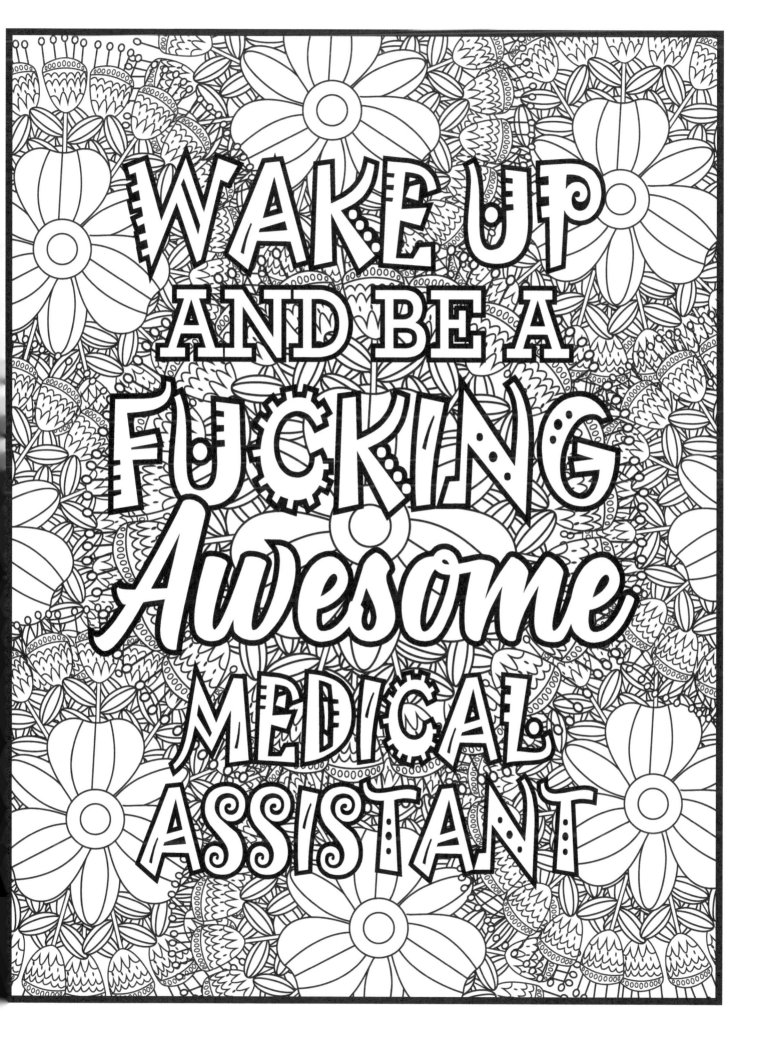

Test Your Colors

THANKS FOR CHOOSING Our COLORING BOOK.
WE TRULY HOPE THE RECIPIENT OF THIS
BOOK GETS A FEW LAUGHS FROM THE QUOTES INSIDE.
AS A SMALL BUSINESS SELLING ON AMAZON,
YOUR FEEDBACK IS IMPORTANT TO US. WE WOULD
APPRECIATEIT IF YOU COULD tAKE A MINUTE TO POST
AN HONEST REVIEW ON AMAZON.

Made in United States
Troutdale, OR
09/19/2024

22947876R00046